Mandala : Adult Coloring Book

Alizabeth J.

Mandala
Coloring For Relax

Published August 2016

ISBN-13:978-1537146980

ISBN-10:153714698X

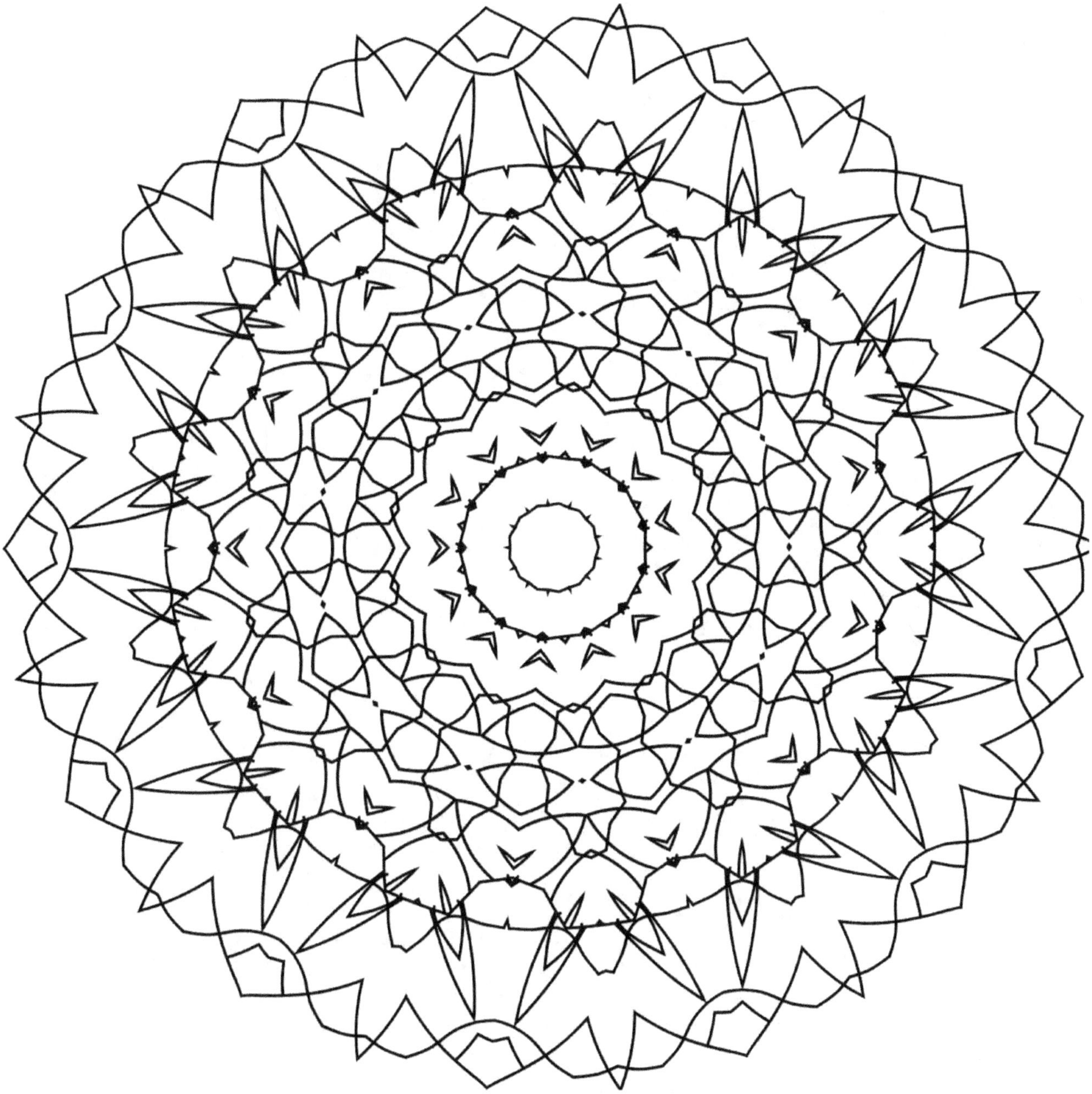

www.ingramcontent.com/pod-product-compliance
Lightning Source LLC
Chambersburg PA
CBHW051950280526
45789CB00009B/3241